A QUESTION AND ANSWER STORYBOOK

Why do Stars Twinkle?

and other nighttime questions

by Catherine Ripley

illustrated by Scot Ritchie

Owl

OWL BOOKS

Why do Stars Twinkle? and other nighttime questions

Owl Books are published by Greey de Pencier Books Inc.,
179 John Street, Suite 500, Toronto, Ontario M5T 3G5

Owl and the Owl colophon are trademarks of Owl Communications.
Greey de Pencier Books Inc. is a licensed user of trademarks of Owl Communications.

Distributed in the United States by Firefly Books (U.S.) Inc.,
230 Fifth Avenue, Suite 1607, New York, NY 10001.

This book was published with the generous support of the Canada Council, the Ontario Arts
Council, and the Ontario Publishing Centre.

Special thanks to the following for their participation in this book: Dr. Randall Brooks, National
Museum of Science and Technology; *Chickadee* magazine; Michel Gosselin, Ornithology Collections,
Canadian Museum of Nature; Dr. Bill James; Cheryl McJannet, Botany Research, Canadian Museum
of Nature; Ontario Arts Council; Dr. and Mrs. Penrose; Susan Woodward, Royal Ontario Museum.
And a big thank you to the people who helped my ideas and words turn into a book complete with lively
pictures full of fun and warmth: Sheba, Kat, Trudee (editors), Mary (art director), and Scot (artist).

DEDICATION

For Mr. Huggins *et al*, especially Mum.

Canadian Cataloguing in Publication Data

Ripley, Catherine, 1957–
Why do stars twinkle? and other nighttime questions

(Question and answer storybooks)
ISBN 1-895688-41-8 (bound) ISBN 1-895688-42-6 (pbk.)

1. Night – Miscellanea – Juvenile literature.
I. Ritchie, Scot. II. Title. III. Series: Ripley,
Catherine, 1957–   . Question and answer
storybooks.

QB633.R56 1996   j525'.3   C95-932574-3

Design and Art Direction: Mary Opper

Also available:
Why is Soap so Slippery? and other bathtime questions
Do the Doors Open by Magic? and other supermarket questions
Why is the Sky Blue? and other outdoor questions

Printed in Hong Kong

A   B   C   D   E   F

Contents

Where does the sun go at night?

It doesn't go anywhere. It looks like it's gone, but it's still shining. We all live on the planet Earth, and it's the Earth — with you on it — that moves. Every day the Earth spins around once. The light from the sun only reaches the part of the Earth closest to it. Daytime happens when the part of the Earth you are on faces the sun. Nighttime happens when your part of the Earth spins away from the sun.

Moon

Sun

Earth

Why do a cat's eyes shine in the dark?

All the better to see with! Way inside a cat's eye are cells that act like a mirror. Light that shines on them is bounced back out. This gives the cat more light to see by in the dark night. When you see a cat's eyes shining in the dark, you are seeing light being reflected back out.

Is there a man in the moon?

Not really. The lines and curves that look like eyes and a nose and a mouth are really mountains and plains on the moon's surface. Moon mountains are made up of light-colored rock. Moon plains are made of dark rock. The bright mountains and dark plains make up the pattern of a man's face in the moon.

Or is it a rabbit?   Or is it a crab?   Or is it a lady?

Why do tulips close up at night?

Because the insides of the flower are very important. That's where new seeds come from. Tulips bloom in spring when nights — brrr! — can be cool and frosty. Cold can hurt the parts inside the flowers, so the flowers close up tight to protect their insides from the cold. When it is warmer during the day, the tulips open up again. Then bees can get inside the flowers to help start new seeds growing. And from new seeds come new flowers.

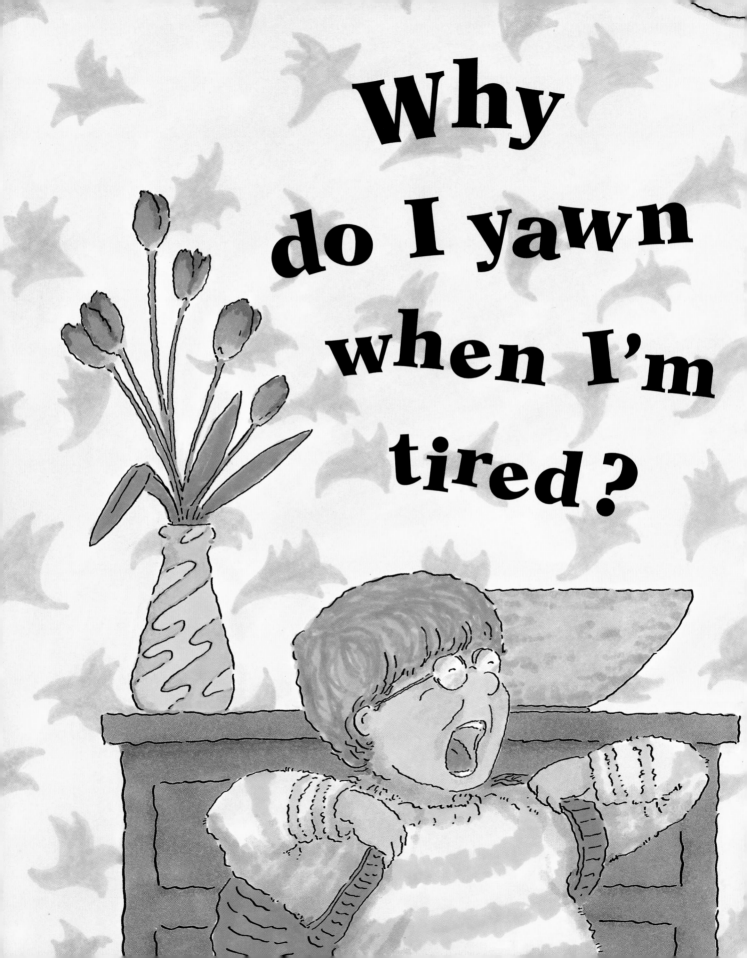

Why do I yawn when I'm tired?

To wake up your brain! To stay active and alert, your brain needs lots of a gas called oxygen. Oxygen is in the air you breathe, and gets sent all around your body in your blood. After a busy day, your heart pumps blood more slowly than before. Your sleepy brain needs more oxygen. YA-A-A-WNNN! You gulp in a lot of air and the oxygen it contains, and your brain feels better.

Why do stars twinkle?

Because of blankets of air. Earth is surrounded by its atmosphere — piles of thin layers or blankets of air. Starlight has to come through the atmosphere for us to see it. It travels in beams from so far away that the beams are weak by the time they get here. They run into humps and bumps in the atmosphere. The light beams move back and forth a little — and the stars seem to wink and twinkle!

Why doesn't that bird fall off the branch?

It is locked into place. Long tendons, or cords, run all the way down the inside of a bird's legs to its toes. To settle on a branch, the bird bends its legs. Bending pulls the tendons. The tendons pull on the toes, making them curl around the branch. As long as the bird is perched on the branch, its legs are bent. As long as its legs are bent, its toes are locked in place.

Tendon

Toes

What's under my bed?

Some toys, a shoe, a book, a sock, . . . and dust mites. Dust mites are tiny creatures so small you can't see them. But if you could shrink down thousands and thousands of times, you'd see dust mites under there, munching away. They chew on tiny flakes of dead skin and loose hair in the dust, and they sure do a good job of cleaning up!

Why do I have to sleep?

No one really knows for sure. Some scientists think you need a time when all the parts of your body can slow down and rest. Others think that sleep also gives your body a chance to make repairs, like healing a cut, and to get back the energy you use during a busy day. Whatever the reason, sleeping must be something you have to do, or you wouldn't get sleepy!

Why can't I see just after the light goes out?

Because your eyes aren't ready for the dark yet. The dark-colored opening in the middle of your eye — the pupil — lets in light so you can see. In the dark, your pupils have to open up wider to catch what little light there is. When the lights first go out, it takes a few seconds for your pupils to widen. Until they do, you can't see much and everything looks completely black.

What makes that toy glow in the dark?

Dancing molecules! All things are made up of tiny bits, called molecules, that are so small you can't see them without a microscope. The toy includes special molecules that get excited by light. Light makes them move and bump and dance. When they bump together, they start to shine. This makes the toy glow. You can see it glow in the dark when the lights go out.

Will I dream tonight?

Absolutely. You dream many, many dreams every single night — even if you don't remember them when you wake up. Scientists think that you dream as your brain tries to make sense of all the things you've done and felt during the day. They also think that animals dream, just like you do. Sweet dreams!

Nighttime Bits

Lots of creatures are busy at night when other animals sleep. After dark, bats come out to catch bugs while daytime birds are snoozing. When daylight comes, bats hang upside-down to sleep while birds fly around catching bugs.

Tick, tick, tick. Even if you can't see a real clock, your body knows it's bedtime at the end of the day. You have a sort of inner clock that senses how much light is around. Less light means it's time to sleep, so your body makes melatonin, a substance that makes you sleepy.

A shooting star isn't a star at all. It's really a meteor, a rock from outer space that burns as it zooms down through the Earth's atmosphere. Flash! Most meteors are pea-sized or smaller, and burn up before they hit the ground.